Book 4

We would learn writing

Written by
Sheila and Ian Spence

Illustrated by David Murray

World

2 Write the letters of the alphabet.

Finish the alphabet.
These are the small letters.

a b c d e f g h i j k l m
n o p q r s t u v w x y z

Write your name in small letters.

....

Finish the alphabet.
These are the big letters.

A B C D E F G H I J K L M
N O P Q R S T U V W X Y Z

Write your name in big letters.

....

a b c d e f g h i j k l m
n o p q r s t u v w x y z

3

Sort these words into the order of the alphabet using the beginning sounds.

ant

deer

lamb

penguin

watch

igloo

a ☐☐
d ☐☐☐
i ☐☐☐
l ☐☐☐
p ☐☐☐☐☐
w ☐☐☐

Finish the patterns across the page. Use different colours.

5 Draw the pictures. Complete the words.

car	spoon
feet	toys
mother	tray

6   ar   or   ee   oo   ay   oy   er

The farm

barn

farmhouse

hay

tractor

sheep

farmer

horse

boy

goose

Complete the words.

7 Add **ee** to complete the words.

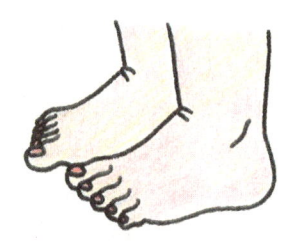

f**ee**t

b _ _

tr _ _

sh _ _ p

sl _ _ p

qu _ _ n

| 8 | **Complete the words.** |

b**oy**

t_o_y_

b**ee**

tr_ _

f**an**

p_ _

st**ar**

c_ _

Read the rhyme.
Match to the correct picture.

a frog on a log

a cat with a hat

a mouse in a house

a fish in a dish

Write the words in the correct order.

help! 10

can swim a fish

a fish can swim

sheep the farmer keeps

....

....

a box blue

....

funny he is

....

11 | **Add oo to complete the words.**

spoon

m_ _n

ball_ _n

kangar_ _

Choose the correct word.

burrow   hand   road   saucer

bird goes with nest

rabbit goes with

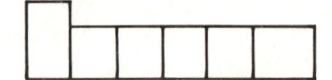

☐☐☐☐☐☐

train goes with track

car goes with

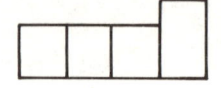

☐☐☐☐

hat goes with head

glove goes with

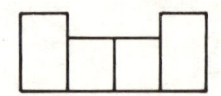

☐☐☐☐

knife goes with fork

cup goes with

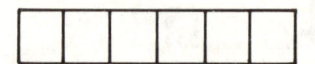

☐☐☐☐☐☐

Look at these pictures.
Draw them in the correct order.

Colour the pictures.

Write a letter to a friend.

Dear

Read the story.

Winnie the 🧙 lives in a 🌲🌲🌲.

She has a  🐈‍⬛ called Tib.

Winnie likes to make spells in a 🍯.

She puts in  🐸 and 🐌.

She puts the  🍯 on her 🔥.

Winnie rides on her  🧹 in the sky.

Find the opposite.

white   down   little   cold

big and l_ _ _ _ _ _

black and w_ _ _ _

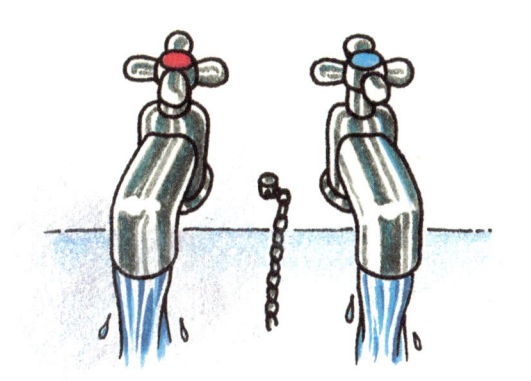

hot and c_ _ _

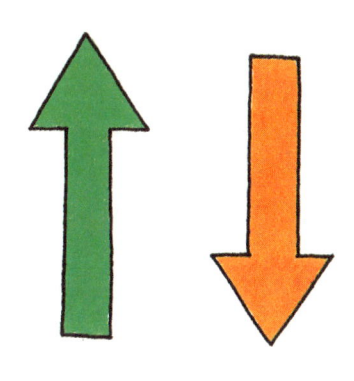

up and d_ _ _

16 Read and draw.

Draw a street.

Draw the pavements.

Draw the houses.

Are there any gardens?

Draw a car in the street.

Colour the picture.

17 What are they doing?

jumping   hopping   swimming   eating

The fish is

_ _ _ _ _ _ _ _

The rabbit is

_ _ _ _ _ _ _ _

The horse is

_ _ _ _ _ _ _ _

The girl is

_ _ _ _ _ _ _ _

Read the words.

star    **dr**ess

brick 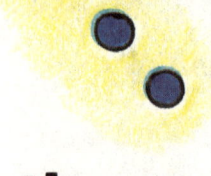   **th**ree

Ring the odd man out.

br   brick   bring   brown   ⊙drink⊙

dr   dress   drop   glass   dry

th   three   cheese   thumb   thin

st   star   stop   song   step

19 Find the words which tell you about the pictures.

tall thin big wet red fat cold hot

the tall, thin man

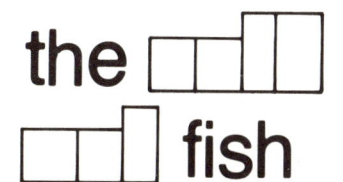

the ☐☐ / ☐☐ cat

the ☐☐☐ / ☐☐ fish

the ☐☐☐ / ☐☐ fire

In the park.

Ring the correct answer.

Where is the lady?

The lady sits on the hill.
The lady sits on a bench.

Where is the dog?

The dog is by the flowers.
The dog is by the tree.

Where is the duck?

The duck is on the pond.
The duck is on the path.

Join the two parts of each sentence.

Jack and Jill   sat in a corner.
Little Jack Horner   she made some tarts.
The queen of hearts   pussy is in the well.
Ding dong bell   went up the hill.

Draw the picture and write the sentence.

Jack and Jill went up the hill.

22 Write the sentences in the correct order.

I go to school.
I get dressed.
I wash myself.
I get out of bed.
I eat my breakfast.

1 _____
2 _____
3 _____
4 _____
5 _____

23 Write yes or no.

The moon shines in the daytime.

☐

Sheep go to town on the bus.

☐

Ships go on the water.

☐

We sleep at night time.

☐

Write what is happening in the pictures. Use these words.

| plane bakes climbs swimming |